SCORNERS AND MOCKERS

SCORNERS AND MOCKERS

HOW TO DAMPEN THEIR INFLUENCE IN YOUR SCHOOL

RICK HORNE

purposeful design
p u b l i c a t i o n s

COLORADO SPRINGS, COLORADO

*Textbooks, Trade Books, and Other Educational Resources
for Christian Educators and Schools Worldwide*

Copyright 2005 by Rick Horne
Published by ACSI/Purposeful Design Publications

Purposeful Design Publications is the publishing division of the Association of
Christian Schools International and is committed to the ministry of Christian school
education, to enable Christian educators and schools worldwide to effectively prepare
students for life. As the publisher of textbooks, trade books, and other educational
resources within ACSI, Purposeful Design Publications strives to produce biblically
sound materials that reflect Christian scholarship and stewardship and that address
the identified needs of Christian schools around the world.

Printed in the United States of America
14 13 12 11 10 09 08 07 06 05   1 2 3 4 5 6 7

ISBN 1-58331-066-5 Catalog #6532

PURPOSEFUL DESIGN PUBLICATIONS
A Division of ACSI

PO Box 65130 • Colorado Springs, CO 80962-5130
Customer Service: 800/367-0798 • Website: www.acsi.org

To my kids' kids,
for
the glory of God

CONTENTS

INTRODUCTION

Christian education is not just Christian teachers teaching from a Christian point of view with biblically principled values and methods. Among other things, it also includes an atmosphere that encourages students to grow.

Conscientious Christian parents want their children to be trained in the discipline and instruction of the Lord, and they want the Christian school experience to aid them with this goal. The spiritual atmosphere of a classroom, grade, or school will either support Christian education or subvert it.

Ron and Anita started their seventh-grade daughter, Angela, in a local Christian middle school. Things seemed to start well, but in the middle of the second quarter, Anita discovered Angela crying in her bedroom. Angela was reluctant to talk about it at first, but she eventually told her mom that the kids at school were mocking her and ignoring her because she was trying to listen in chapel and to show interest in her Bible class.

Anita thought there must be more to it and called several of Angela's teachers the next day. Anita found that Angela's grades and homework were going fine. Teachers thought Angela was getting along well with a couple of the other girls in her classes but that her cheerfulness and willingness to participate in classes had diminished. Several teachers did affirm that there were a number of guys and a couple of girls in Angela's grade who seemed to throw a spiritual wet blanket on everything positive that the teachers tried to do or say. They suspected, as Angela had said, that some of these students actively put her and others down when they tried to listen or answer questions in classes—especially during discussions about the Bible and spiritual things.

After they began to give further attention to these students, they noticed that these were the same kids who would sit in the back of chapel and make comments under their breath throughout the worship times. "Their body language screams that they are not really listening and that they couldn't care less," one of the teachers confessed. "But we just can't pin any specific offense on any of them. They are very subtle around teachers. They seem to wield a powerful influence in Angela's grade, but they don't break any rules so we can't discipline them. The ones with the most negative attitudes get good grades, so the administration doesn't know what to do with them. They roll their eyes, smirk, and make comments that only the closest students can hear and laugh about. We just pray about these kids and trust the Lord to change them."

Scorners, as the Bible describes them, are not necessarily students who are intellectually dull or who are socially acting out. They wield a power, however, that is disproportionate to their numbers. These are the students who can transform a classroom, a grade, and even an entire school in one day by just being absent: "Dead flies make the perfumer's ointment give off a stench, so a little folly outweighs wisdom and honor" (Ecclesiastes 10:1). A few of these students can have more than a little impact in a school where many teachers model true wise living, godliness, and skillful teaching. In fact, in Solomon's estimation, it will "outweigh" the virtues that godly, conscientious teachers and administrators in Christian schools want in order to control the school's esprit de corps. Throughout this book, I will use the terms *scorners, mockers,* and *scoffers* interchangeably to refer to these students.

This book is about bringing these powerful students in check. It is about how the Scriptures both urge and command Christian leaders and parents to hold these young people accountable for their "intangible" or elusive attitudes, not just their more readily seen behaviors. When a school applies these principles, "the simple will learn prudence" (Proverbs 19:25), and an easily influenced student "becomes wise" (Proverbs 21:11). After these students have been dealt with as the Scriptures command, teachers have approached me with tears in their eyes, talking about the transformation of their classes, their schools, and their own spiritual vitality and even the return of their old enthusiasm for teaching.

One final introductory caution: Solomon observes, "The poor use entreaties, but the rich answer roughly" (Proverbs 18:23). Taking action with these destructive students will take resolve. But we must not allow the "power" of our position to clothe our resolve with the arrogant or callous spirit of the "rich." Our posture should be more like that of the poor. We have reason to entreat these young people with a spirit of meekness, for we are weak people too. Decisions and actions must be taken if we are to be obedient to the Lord with these students, but the attitude with which we do that is as important as the process itself. I hope this spirit of meekness characterizes my treatment of the subject. If I fall short of that goal, it will be because of my lack of sensitivity to my own weaknesses, to God's love for me, and to my need to love these students as I have been loved.

THE IMPACT AND INFLUENCE OF SCORNERS AND MOCKERS

Scorners and mockers are not necessarily the students who are most influential in getting others to smoke, drink, use drugs, lie, or cheat. Their impact is actually more serious than that. It is attitudinal. Attitudes shape the character and spirit of the classroom, the students' willingness to learn and take seriously a Christian worldview in any subject area, and even the zeal of teachers and leaders of the school.

More specifically, as we saw with seventh-grader Angela in the introduction, scorners and mockers can wield a power that may discourage spiritually concerned students. But they can also sow the seeds of discord, embolden others to display contempt or indifference for righteous attitudes, and even demoralize teachers and others in the contexts of school or church ministry.

Strife, Quarreling, Anger, and Abuse

Solomon acknowledges this impact with his stern counsel to "drive out a scoffer." Do so, he says, and "strife will go out, and quarreling and abuse will cease" (Proverbs 22:10). Scorners spawn all three of these. Their values center on themselves. Scorners and mockers have contempt for God and His authority and anyone who represents or is sensitive to or is respectful of His authority. Scorners and mockers will cause division because they will not cooperate with anyone who stifles their will or authority. They want to be in control or have things go in the spiritually disinterested way in which they want them to go. This spirit brings them into conflict with students who have a spirit of respect, a willingness to learn and grow, and an interest in God and His purposes. It also gives them a spirit of contempt for teachers or others who want to bring God's authority to the forefront of decision making or classroom discussions. Scorners and mockers are impatient with that concern. Their attitudes yield an atmosphere of strife, argumentativeness, anger, and verbal and nonverbal disrespect.

A student named Bill used to come to sophomore class meetings, sit in the back row with a few friends, and make continual under-the-breath comments that his buddies laughed at. None of them paid serious or even polite attention to the students who were trying to lead the class meeting. When Steve, the president of the class, tried to suggest something or listen to ideas of his classmates, Bill and his friends usually made negative comments or just sneered and laughed: "That's stupid! We don't want to do that. We're not gonna come." After hearing these comments, the rest of the class began to make fewer suggestions or comments. A few other class members, in another part of the room but within earshot of Bill, would become emboldened to echo some of the same negative sentiments. Instead of thinking about how they could make the class plans work, these students were critics and detractors from any ideas that classmates suggested. At first, the naysayers spoke quietly. As the meeting went on, though, they became more and more vocal. They used words, of course, but their attitudes were also written all over their faces or were evident in the tone of their voices. Steve, the class president, was frustrated. Other interested class members became dispirited, and the class advisors were exasperated.

"Scoffers set a city aflame, but the wise turn away wrath" (Proverbs 29:8). Scoffers are not necessarily the majority of any group, but their disproportionate influence, if left unchecked, is such that they can affect the whole "city," whomever that group may be. Solomon provided a vivid metaphor in Ecclesiastes 10:1. He said, "Dead flies make the perfumer's ointment give off a stench, so a little folly outweighs wisdom and honor." Tolerating even a little folly can create a stench that permeates a much larger venue. Solomon referred to the insidious nature of "little foxes" let loose to run through "vineyards … in blossom." The immediate context is the rich intimacy between him and his bride. He urged, "Catch the foxes for us, the little foxes that spoil the vineyards" (Song of Solomon 2:15). The vineyard of relationships within a class, grade, or even a school can be spoiled by "little foxes." Paul also described the influence of an arrogant spirit when he said that a "little yeast works through the whole batch of dough" (1 Corinthians 5:6, NIV).

The power opposition by scoffers is brought into bright focus in Psalm 69 (a Messianic psalm) when the Messiah testifies to the impact of reproaches hurled at Him. "You know my reproach, and my shame and my dishonor; my foes are all known to you. Reproaches have broken my heart, so that I am in despair" (19–20). The New International Version translates these reproaches as scorn that has broken His heart and left Him helpless. The personal testimony of the perfect, sovereign Son of God, in His humanity, was that scorn was crushingly deadening. If that is the impact it makes on Him, we should not be surprised at the influence it has on weaker, inconsistent, and younger, believing or unbelieving young people who may have had an open, teachable spirit at one time. Scorners and mockers, though a minority, can "stir up" strife, anger, quarrels, and an insulting, cynical spirit toward anything good that we want to see happen within the school community.

2

THE CHARACTER OF SCORNERS AND MOCKERS

Whoever corrects a scoffer gets himself abuse, and he who reproves a wicked man incurs injury. Do not reprove a scoffer, or he will hate you; reprove a wise man, and he will love you. (Proverbs 9:7–8)

A wise son hears his father's instruction, but a scoffer does not listen to rebuke. (Proverbs 13:1)

A scoffer does not like to be reproved; he will not go to the wise. (Proverbs 15:12)

In the last chapter, we looked at the deadening influence of the scoffer. But where does all this power to sow discord, discouragement, and contempt come from? Jesus explained that it is "out of the abundance of the heart the mouth speaks" (Matthew 12:34). The spirit that one radiates by his or her words, tone, and body language emerges from the kind of person that he or she is. This chapter summarizes some of the major brushstrokes with which the Bible paints the character of scorners. If we are going to deal with these young people effectively, we need to know what they look like. We will go into many of the specific common verbal and nonverbal behaviors of scorners later in this chapter. First, we will note the major themes the Bible uses to describe the scorner's character and corresponding behavior.

The Age of "It's Not My Fault"

We live in an age in which it is common to blame others for our attitudes and behaviors. This blame shifting shows up in the scoffer too:

- He makes me so angry!
- She's upsetting me. That's why I'm so negative.
- These teachers are just trying to ram God-stuff down our throats, and that's what I'm sick of.
- This school su_ _ _! I'm not going to pretend it doesn't. I'm just being honest.
- He is always preaching to us about how God wants us to think about things in history. Why can't the teachers just teach their subjects? Why do they have to bring God into everything?
- I'm not one of the "favorites." That's why the teacher is always talking about my attitude. I don't kiss up to her like some of the "good" kids do.
- These kids in my class all think they are so perfect. I'm not going to be a hypocrite like them. So, I just say what I think.

My words and attitudes are my choices. Though it is not a popular concept, the fact is, I cannot blame anyone else for my spirit. In the next chapter, we will see how the Bible affirms that attitudes are truly chosen. They do not "happen" to us. We will also consider how the Bible holds young people accountable for their chosen attitudes. The focus of this chapter, however, is to summarize what the Bible says these people are really like at heart—the source of bad fruit (Luke 6:43–45) or the fountain of this bitter salt water (James 3:11).

Scoffers Do Not Respond Well to Correction

All three passages at the beginning of this chapter declare scoffers' unwillingness to hear rebuke, instruction, correction, or reproof. The character of scoffers is most clearly viewed when they are confronted about their attitudes (or any area of sin). And it really does not matter how gently these things are brought up to them.

In a sense, these passages are prophetic. It does not matter how prayerful you are, how much preparation you give to the confrontation, how kindly you speak, or how meekly and humbly you approach the topic. Given their spirit and attitudes, scoffers, when confronted in even the most gracious manner, will reject the point if they get it. Most often, they will react as Proverbs 9 predicts, with insults, abuse, and hatred. Usually, these are of a nonverbal nature.

In addition, these students are not going to accept your wise, loving concern and then approach you for help. As Proverbs 15:12 says in the New International Version, they will not "consult the wise." All your praying will not bring these students into a posture of humble submission. A scorner will not be coming to you in tears confessing, "I have been such a scorner. My attitude stinks. Please forgive me. I've made it tough for other kids here and for you in the classroom. This is sin, and I recognize it. Please help me get this spirit under control."

Proverbs 1:22 asks, "How long will scoffers delight in their scoffing?" There is a payoff for scoffing. Mockers have a self-deluded sense of power over one or over many. They get to be their own gods—at least in the authority they think they are wielding. They can undermine the seriousness of a teacher, neutralize the challenges of a chapel speaker, confound the efforts of class leaders or activity organizers, and sour the general atmosphere of positiveness and enthusiasm for a good cause.

There is a reason scorners behave as they do. It is not because prayer *doesn't work* or because a teacher is not gracious enough or because the school has not been patient enough. A meek response will not be forthcoming from the scorner because of the kind of person the scorner has chosen to be. As a comparison, the Lord's passionate, loving appeals to the lost, which were met with disdain and mockery, did not mean that the gospel *didn't work* or that Jesus was an ineffective witness. These reactions just showed that people are real and that they make real choices. Scorners are the same way. They get something out of holding on to this spirit. They find "delight" in their "scoffing." It is worth it to them, for the time being, to be this way.

A Pattern of Criticism, Negativity, and Passivity

One of the most common telltale signs that a teacher is dealing with students who are scorners or mockers is the reaction the teacher gets when correcting these students. The problem is not that the teacher is unfair, even if the teacher may be unfair at times. It is not that the teacher has boring methods, even though his or her classes may not always be the most interesting classes. It is not that the teacher is ramming "God-stuff" down the students' throats. It is not "the stupid school rules." Scoffing comes from choices that the young people make about the authorities who are confronting them at the moment. These reactions come from hearts that want something different.

> Scoffers will come in the last days with scoffing, following their own sinful desires. (2 Peter 3:3)

> Blessed is the man who walks not in the counsel of the wicked, nor stands in the way of sinners, nor sits in the seat of scoffers. (Psalm 1:1)

A scoffer is not someone who simply scoffs. Scoffing is a pattern of living. As can be seen in the following story, everyone can have a bad day and can react sinfully with a scornful attitude toward others, events, and even the Lord. But this is not who the Bible depicts to be a scoffer.

> Sarah got up late. She was looking for a special green shirt to wear. She had been planning to wear it today because of what her friends were going to wear, but she could not find it. She ran downstairs and hollered for her mom.
> "Mom, do you know where my green shirt is?"
>
> "Yes, Honey. It's in the dirty laundry. You didn't bring it down earlier in the week, and I noticed it in your laundry basket when I gathered the dirty laundry yesterday. I'll be washing it today."
>
> More than a little annoyed, Sarah groaned as she ran back upstairs. Soon she came rushing down the steps again,

dressed and ready to pick up her book bag and head out the door.

"Wait, Young Lady," her mom said. "You need something to eat before heading to the bus."

"But Mom, I'll be late."

"No, you won't," her mother insisted. "At least take this toast with you and eat it on the way."

Sarah turned toward the door now, with toast and book bag in hand, and her mother stopped her again.

"You can't go out like that, Sarah. It's thirty-five degrees outside."

"Mom, I'm OK. Nobody is wearing coats yet."

"Put your coat on, Sarah, and get moving to the bus stop."

Sarah put her toast and book bag down, put on her coat, picked up her toast and book bag again, and headed off to the bus stop, with no loving thoughts streaming through her mind. She was upset.

On the bus, Sarah's friend Kim asked her if she was ready for the math test. "Oh, no! I totally forgot about it. Is that really today? Can I use your notes to look at them on the bus?"

When the bus pulled up to the school, Sarah got off to be greeted by Carey and Tina, who were not really Sarah's good friends. They were both grinning and eager to talk to Sarah, and they went right up to her. With a sneering tone in her voice, Carey said, "Sarah, did you hear that Bill [the guy Sarah was going out with] was at the mall last night with Erin?"

Sarah turned away, with her heart swinging between anger and ache. She went to her locker, and it seemed to take longer than usual for her to get her things for the morning classes. She rushed down the hall, headed for homeroom. Just as she got to the door, the bell rang.

"Sarah, you are late! That will mean a detention."

Sarah stomped to her desk, slammed her books down, and dropped into the desk chair, angry, annoyed, and glaring at Mr. Lewis.

Was Sarah a scorner? She was not in the strictest sense of the term. She was angry, upset, and disrespectful. All these areas would have to be addressed, and sin would have to be dealt with, but this behavior was not a pattern for Sarah. She was being buried by an avalanche of troubles she had to face even before her first class of the day.

In the Bible, scorning is pictured as a pattern of behaviors that reflects an attitude of contempt toward the authorities in one's life—God especially, but also anyone who gets in one's face with God's demands. For a young person, the authorities could be teachers, chapel speakers, administrators, parents, youth workers, pastors, or peers. The passage above from 2 Peter depicts scoffing as a lifestyle. Psalm 1:1 uses an interesting phrase to describe a significant feature of this person. A godly person, David affirms, does not sit "in the seat of scoffers." The scoffer sits. Passivity is the scoffer's pattern, being a critic rather than being an active, constructive participant in something. He or she is passive in everything except attitude and negativity. The scoffer is aggressively hurtful in these areas.

This is not the place to get into an extended discussion about the "last days" in which Peter says this scorning will be so insidious. Suffice it to say that whatever else the apostles had in mind with that term, they understood this current age to be the last days (see Hebrews 6:4–12, 2 Timothy 3:1, 1 John 2:18–19) in which this troublesome spirit would be destructively present. For as long as Satan seductively appeals to us as he did to Adam and Eve when he asserted, "You will be like God" (Genesis 3:5), we will be tempted to dismiss and hold God's authority in contempt in order to establish our own. Every scornful disposition is that effort in its most naked form.

Scorning can appear in both nonverbal and verbal forms. Before I list these, it is important to repeat that not one, or even two, of these things makes a scorner. It is critical to observe a pattern of these behaviors, a pattern that reflects the disposition that is so discouraging, divisive, and caustic to a community.

Common Nonverbal and Verbal Communication Patterns of the Scoffer

Renowned seminary professor and Christian educator Howard Hendricks has cited research findings which show that 7 percent of our communication is through the words we use, 38 percent is through the tone of our voice, and 55 percent is through our body language, or nonverbal communication. Scorners are often masters of this last form of communication. In a school setting, there are few rules against such nonverbal communication. Scoffers know how to speak volumes of disrespect and contempt without saying a word or breaking a rule.

Nonverbal Styles
- rolling eyes
- a sigh, a breath of disgust/contempt
  (often accompanies the rolling eyes)
- the silent treatment when being addressed
- avoidance of eye contact when being spoken to
- a smirk or patronizing smile
- stubbornness
- an angry glare
- slouching defiance
- disruptive, annoying noises

Verbal Styles
- deceit
- nasty speech
- arrogant tone of voice
- uncooperativeness
- hateful tones and words
- contempt
- patronizing speech

.ory speech

᠎defiance
• insulting speech
• slander
• the disrespectful "why" that is not really a question but a statement about how stupid or unreasonable you are
• sneering speech, derisive speech
• belittling, rude name calling or labeling

In the appendix, you will find a chart that may be copied and used to help identify the scorners or mockers in your school. I recommend that you have a faculty or group discussion about the nature and character of scorners and mockers before you use it. The pattern nature of this offense in contrast to more random incidents of scorning or scoffing must be stressed.

In Matthew 7:2, Jesus made it plain that judgment we exercise needs to be humble and gracious. The measure of strictness that we use will be used against us. This verse does not mean that we may not assess attitudes of young people. We will see in a later chapter that some who defend scorners (often parents) abuse this passage by using it to get the administrator or teacher off a child's case. They have misunderstood what Jesus is saying in this passage. He is affirming that when judgments do have to be made, they must be made with humility and grace. This passage will be examined in more detail in chapter 5.

Some teachers have asked how old a student might be before he or she exhibits these attitude patterns. Although not the most common time for this spirit to be displayed, sadly, children as young as those in the primary grades have been reported to manifest it. However, it is seen more often in the middle school and high school years.

Wherever it is found, there is a price to be paid for ignoring this attitude. Action must be taken.

THE ACCOUNTABILITY OF
SCORNERS AND MOCKERS

Teens are young adults! As such, they are accountable for
their choices.

In this chapter, I will identify some of the biblical evidence which
shows that God holds young people accountable for "intangible"
or elusive attitudes (not just their more readily definable behaviors) that they choose to display. Similarly, the authority figures
(the adults) in the lives of young people must hold the young people accountable because of the adults' own accountability and love
for the Lord and the teen. In the next chapter, I will further
underscore this teaching by identifying two underlying presuppositions that the Scriptures teach as the foundation for holding any
young person accountable for his or her choices.

God Commands Action, Not Just Talk, as the Antidote to Scornful Young People

1. Strike a scoffer, and the simple will learn prudence;
   reprove a man of understanding, and he will gain
   knowledge. (Proverbs 19:25)

Notice the contrast in the above verse. The scoffer is not predicted
to change. As we saw in the last chapter, his or her character
rejects culpability: "It's your fault I'm this way" or "What rule
have I broken? I'm not a scorner! That's your opinion." In the

above verse, Solomon urges the adult to bring pain of one sort or another into the scoffer's life. A Hebrew wordplay illustrates the way the rabbis thought one should treat the wise and the scoffer: "For the wise a hint, for the fool a fist" (Ross 1991, 1037). Commentator Derek Kidner shows the mind-sets of three different kinds of people in this verse. He writes about the closed, empty, and open (1964, 135). These correspond to the scoffer, the simple, and the person of understanding or discernment.

The significant thing to note about Solomon's counsel is that he asserts that action, not anger, threats, or reasoning, is the way to work with the scorner—"the closed," in Kidner's terms. If we work with the scorner in this way, it does not mean that we should exclude explanations and efforts to reason with such a young person. But, true to character, he or she will not be responsive to these approaches. Action is required.

>   2. When a scoffer is punished, the simple becomes wise;
>   when a wise man is instructed, he gains knowledge.
>   (Proverbs 21:11)

This passage assumes that punishment comes to the mocker or scoffer. It is not a question of *if* such a response will be necessary, only *when.* (As with the last verse, there are often spin-off effects for the simple, naive, or uncommitted. I will refer to some of these in the last chapter when we look at the most significant and yet typical outcomes of faithfully dealing with the scoffer.)

>   3. Drive out a scoffer, and strife will go out, and quarreling
>   and abuse will cease. (Proverbs 22:10)

We referred to this verse when we talked about the scoffer's effects in chapter 1. Notice the action in this verse that precludes compromise with the scoffer: drive out the scoffer. Any plan to see change in a school's atmosphere that is being affected by a scoffer must include a heartbreaking but definitive dismissal as a real disciplinary consequence. In chapter 5, we will address some of the relevant biblical wisdom for going in this direction. For now, it will suffice to see that this weapon is a vital option for this spiritual warfare.

Action Is the Response for the New Testament Community Too

4. I appeal to you, brothers, to watch out for those who cause divisions and create obstacles contrary to the doctrine that you have been taught; avoid them. For such persons do not serve our Lord Christ, but their own appetites. (Romans 16:17–18)

As for a person who stirs up division, after warning him once and then twice, have nothing more to do with him, knowing that such a person is warped and sinful; he is self-condemned. (Titus 3:10–11)

Both of the passages above are in the context of church discipline. Our schools are not churches, but Paul's counsel for handling these people is applicable. He says to "avoid them" and "have nothing more to do with [them]."

One of the insidious effects of the scorner or mocker is divisiveness. He or she causes contention, strife, and quarrels (Proverbs 22:10). A mocker or scorner can set a city aflame with anger (Proverbs 29:8)! Paul, in his epistle to Pastor Titus, instructs him to take action regarding these people. Likewise, Paul urges the church in Rome to go out of their way to not be influenced by them. He says to "avoid them."

These people that the Bible is referring to had destructive attitudes. Their words contributed to their disruptive impact, but their attitudes were just as poisonous. Again, those to whom Paul was writing were to take action. They were not to just send them off to a counselor for six months of therapy. Even in New Testament times, when believers were to display "love, which binds everything together in perfect harmony" (Colossians 3:14), the church was to apply stern measures. This was a command. God is long-suffering, and believers are to be long-suffering. However, displaying love does not preclude holding people accountable for their noxious choices.

TWO BIBLICAL PRESUPPOSITIONS THAT UNDERLIE OUR EFFORTS TO HOLD SCORNERS AND MOCKERS ACCOUNTABLE

Youth, teens in particular, are young adults in biblical terms.

Adolescence as a separate or distinct stage does not exist in a biblical paradigm of teen development. This does not mean that some of the features that typically accompany the teen experience are not acknowledged in Scripture. The Bible, the wisdom literature especially, has a great deal to say about young people and the tasks they need to address. But our modern category of adolescence, affected more by psychological doctrine than biblical concepts, often minimizes the accountability and responsibility of teens. The modern notion is that nothing really "counts" during this stage. Teens are exploring and experimenting. They are just preparing for adulthood, when life and their decisions really will count. This may be an extreme way to summarize the spirit of our age, but it is not too far out of sync with the typical educational profile of teens and the popular advice given to parents about raising them: Life does not really matter at this stage. After you get out of college, get a job, have a spouse, and get settled in a home, then life is really serious.

The Bible says much about young people, but in this book, we will only focus on two of its presuppositions about youth, presuppositions that most significantly have an impact on our responsibility to address scorners and mockers.

1. Youth are young adults who are accountable for their choices.

The Hebrew word for a young person who is not really a child or a fully mature adult is *na'ar*. Used more than 250 times in the Old Testament, it usually refers to young people from puberty to the late twenties. These young people are considered "young adults." The New International Version (NIV) usually translates the word as "young men" or "youth." The English Standard Version (ESV) commonly uses "boy," "young," "young man," or "youth." This is not simply wordplay to differentiate it from the modern concept *adolescent*. Note the accountability, the realness of choices that the na'ar makes in the verses discussed below.

In Lot's hometown of Sodom, "the men of the city … both young [na'ar] and old, all the people to the last man, surrounded the house" (Genesis 19:4). Genesis says the people who surrounded the house wanted to have sexual relations with the male guests whom Lot was hosting. Lot did not know that his guests were angelic beings. When the men of the city continued to put pressure on Lot to give up his guests to them, the angels "struck with blindness the men who were at the entrance of the house, both small and great, so that they wore themselves out groping for the door" (Genesis 19:11). The young and old were held accountable for their lusts.

"Joseph, being seventeen years old, was pasturing the flock with his brothers. He was a boy [na'ar] with the sons of Bilhah and Zilpah" (Genesis 37:2). Joseph, as a seventeen-year-old, is noted to be a na'ar, and as the story unfolds, he goes on to make decisions and have reactions that bring further negative and positive consequences into his life. His choices are real.

When Samuel was identifying the next king of Israel, after Saul had disqualified himself and his family line, Samuel came to Jesse's home. "Then Samuel said to Jesse, 'Are all your sons here?' And he said, 'There remains yet the youngest [na'ar], but behold, he is keeping the sheep' " (1 Samuel 16:11). Not too much later, when Saul wanted someone to play music for him to quiet him, one of his servants said, "Behold, I have seen a son of Jesse the Bethlehemite, who is skillful in playing, a man of valor, a man of war, prudent in speech, and a man of good presence, and the LORD is with him" (1 Samuel 16:18). He is a young man but one who is still referred to as a man.

Still later, in the setting in which Goliath challenges the Israelites, Saul said to the volunteer David, "You are not able to go against this Philistine to fight with him, for you are but a youth [na'ar]" (1 Samuel 17:33). The fact that he was a youth even insults Goliath: "And when the Philistine looked and saw David, he disdained him, for he was but a youth [na'ar]" (1 Samuel 17:42).

"How can a young man [na'ar] keep his way pure? By guarding it according to your word" (Psalm 119:9). Notice how na'ar can make real decisions about purity and guarding themselves against immorality.

Most significant, though, is the prologue of Proverbs in which all the counsel of Proverbs is noted to be for na'ar. The wisdom of the proverbs of Solomon is "to give prudence to the simple, knowledge and discretion to the youth [na'ar]" (1:4).

Consider the range of choices that the readers of Proverbs were to think about: choices involving work and laziness, friendships, relationships with women, respect for authority, responses to correction, use of money, trust and pride, fear, planning for the future, listening to others, observing the wisdom and folly of others, anger, blame shifting, making excuses, confessing wrongdoing, diligence, drunkenness, and many other "adult" behaviors that have positive or negative outcomes. The incentives for making wise choices are given in nearly seven hundred positive or negative consequences that are connected to counsel throughout the book. Young people were just as liable to these outcomes as older adults were. Accountability is real for choices that na'ar make.

Youth, adolescents, teens, young people—whatever label one wants to use for these people—are "young adults." Even today, the Jewish community continues to celebrate bar mitzvah as a transition from childhood to manhood for Jewish boys. To shed more light on the use of the word *na'ar,* consider that the term *na'ar* is sometimes even translated "slave" because of what young adults and slaves have in common. They both have all the capabilities and accountability of free, full adults, but neither has the total freedom of free, full adults. They are still under authority.

The young people we work with are real decision makers. The Bible affirms that they are decision makers and, just as certainly, affirms that they are accountable for choices they make. For purposes of this book, these choices include the attitudes that they adopt.

> 2. Scripture asserts that scornful attitudes are among the behaviors that young people choose and are accountable for: "The eye that mocks a father and scorns to obey a mother will be picked out by the ravens of the valley and eaten by the vultures." (Proverbs 30:17)

Notice what is doing the scorning or mocking in this verse: the eye. Nonverbal attitudes that are communicated by body language are still messages for which young people are accountable. Some of the most powerful scorning that is done by young people is done without an audible word. The eyes say it all.

Photographs of witnesses who want to remain anonymous in television interviews often have the eyes blocked out. Eyes and identity often go together. We recognize each other often by looking at the eyes of the people we see. Similarly, eyes communicate powerfully. In his early days, Yasir Arafat was an avowed terrorist, and he insisted on wearing dark glasses in all his public appearances. When asked about this habit by a reporter, he is reputed to have said that if he covered up his eyes, no one could tell whether he was telling the truth. The eyes speak. And the eyes of the scorner or mocker speak volumes. In the above verse from Proverbs, God notes this contemptible form of speech—scorning or mocking with the eyes—and depicts a gruesome consequence to show His abhorrence for those who "speak" it.

In 2 Kings, the Lord again affirms the seriousness of attitudes that young people (na'ar) choose. Elisha was going to Bethel, a city that had an ancient history as a center of worship. Bethel is the place where Jacob had met the Lord: "So Jacob called the name of the place where God had spoken with him Bethel" (Genesis 35:15). But things had deteriorated in Israel by the time of Elisha. As he came to the town, "some small boys [na'ar] came out of the city and jeered at him, saying, 'Go up, you baldhead! Go up, you baldhead!' And he turned around, and when he saw them, he cursed them in the name of the LORD. And two she-bears came out of the woods and tore forty-two of the boys [na'ar]" (2 Kings 2:23–25).

These young people probably did not get this attitude of contempt for a man of God from thin air. They probably picked it up from the things their parents said. There seems to be more here than simply some innocent kids having fun with a bald-headed man. There is contempt for the prophet of the Lord. That is why God honors the curse and sends out the two bears to maul the na'ar. Young people may be influenced by their parents, and they may imitate what they have seen and heard, but young people are responsible for their own attitudes toward God and His servant.

Many factors may make it easy for young people to choose a scornful attitude. No factor, however, *makes* them choose it. Factors such as their learning disability needs, socioeconomic situation, single-parent home environment, background of abuse, separated or divorced parents, or poor self-esteem do not force young people to be scorners. Most teachers and pastors have known children and adults who have had one or more of these difficulties and yet have exhibited a sweetness and grace that comes from the Spirit's work in them. Circumstances do not *make* someone choose to be bitter, resentful, hateful, or scornful. Circumstances may make it easier to make that choice than if these situations were not true in their lives. But the young person still makes the choice.

A number of years ago, I was part of a faculty and student talent show in our school. I played a villain in a little comedy melodrama. We rehearsed in a classroom. At first, none of the props that we would use in the play had been made available to us. I used a piece of chalk for my knife and an eraser for my pistol. I pretended to tie up my victims with an imaginary rope. When we finally did get to rehearse with the scenery as a backdrop, instead of a blackboard, and with real props, I found it much easier to get in character, probably because I am not much of an actor. The staging helped me accept the role more easily.

The same is true of our young people who come to us from diffi-cult home situations or troubled histories. Their backgrounds are the staging that may make it easy for some of them to become angry and cynical or scornful and bitter toward God and other authorities in their lives, but their backgrounds do not *cause* that spirit. A scornful spirit is a chosen set of attitudes. Scorners choose to accept the invitation that sin offers them—to think that they deserve something different from what life or God is dishing out to them. They think they are entitled to something different: to be treated differently, to not have to listen to the teacher talk about God, to not have to put up with the school's rules, to not have to allow the teacher to be in charge and tell them what to do.

Scornful, bitter attitudes do not *happen* to young people. Young people are not innocent bystanders who are struck by some atmos-pheric spirit in their homes that overwhelms them and makes them the way they are. I do not mean to minimize the trauma of some of the tragic and disadvantageous experiences many of our students have in this fallen world. Many of us weep, at least in our hearts, for the remarkably horrible situations that some of our stu-dents come from, day by day. It amazes me sometimes that some of our kids can put one foot in front of the other without distrac-tion. We need to offer support, love, and practical help to these young people in any way the Lord makes it possible. But their chosen spirit or attitude of contempt for the authority of God or another, which shows up in a scornful or scoffing attitude, must be addressed as sin. They are not victims in this regard. God treats this choice as contemptible, and we must do so as well.

A PROCESS FOR HOLDING SCORNERS AND MOCKERS ACCOUNTABLE: SOME PROCEDURAL WISDOM

> Strike a scoffer, and the simple will learn prudence.
> (Proverbs 19:25)

From the passages we have looked at in the previous chapters, it is clear that God commands us to address scorners with firmness. In our schools, we do not literally "flog" (NIV) or "strike" (ESV) them as the sage of Proverbs directed the community to do in the passage above. But the message we are commanded to send should communicate that this spirit is just as unwelcome in our school communities as it was in Old Testament times.

This chapter suggests some ideas to keep in mind when we identify and confront the scoffer and his or her parents about the need for change. It also sketches some broad strokes of a process to graciously, though firmly, bring specific and painful consequences into the scoffer's life when that change is not forthcoming.

The Scene . . .

It is November. It has taken you a while to come to the conclusion that you may have a scoffer on your hands, but you now believe so. Your mild corrections, positive encouragements, and casual rebukes to Tom during class have gone unheeded. In fact, you have been troubled by what has grown, in your mind, to look like a spirit of defiance. As your awareness has become more vivid, you have carefully and prayerfully logged Tom's behaviors that communicate this attitude. He holds you, others, and God's values and authority in contempt. And he shows it. You have noted how his influence in the class is like that of the scoffer in Proverbs. When he is present, the class is weighed down with a spirit of tenseness because of his under-the-breath criticalness and complaining. When he is absent, the class has a completely different air. With the under-the-breath put-downs that seem to profusely flow from him, he is able to spread a wet blanket on the enthusiasm or positive spirit of others who do want to participate.

You know it is time to speak to him directly about your concern. You know this could be the first of a series of straightforward talks with Tom, other teachers, his parents, and the administrator that could make the next few months very uncomfortable. No one wants to be perpetually bludgeoned by an attitude club that is often wielded and hidden again before it can be clearly seen, grasped, or restrained. Unless the Lord intervenes, Tom is not going to receive what you have to say, and things may get worse before they get better.

But Cheer Up—Things May Get Worse More Quickly Than You Thought

The problem may be bigger than Tom. Any teacher who has had more than a few parent-teacher conferences knows how a defensive parent can compound the obstacles a student must overcome. Just as painful, though, and with longer-lasting invisible bruises, are the charges, innuendos, and even threats that a parent may hurl at or insinuate about a teacher who is trying to address attitudes of the student. More than rarely, it is sad to say, a scornful young person may be imitating his or her parents' attitude. It may be, as the Swedish proverb says, that the "apple does not fall far from the tree."

The appearance of this threat can certainly add to the temptation for any of us to sweep these concerns under the carpet. But God's directives about action in the scoffer's life are not suggestions.

Love for the Lord, the student, and our other students demands that we take action. In the final analysis, young people make their own choices about the attitudes they are going to display. As we saw in the last chapter, they must be held accountable for their attitudes—regardless of how mom or dad reacts. Chronic needs, bad parent examples, and serious disadvantages may give students occasions to be negative, but that is far different from saying that these difficult experiences *cause* young people to display the attitude that God says He "hates" (Proverbs 6:16–19, 8:13, 16:5, 21:4).

A Common Charge from Angry Parents

We have already seen that scorners do not willingly receive correction or instruction. That may be true of their parents also. Commonly, when teachers have begun to address these concerns with parents, they get such reactions as, "You are judging my child, and the Bible says, 'judge not.' It seems to me that you people in this school are the ones who have the attitude problem. What right do you have to judge? You are the ones ignoring the Bible!" This charge can, at the very least, be unsettling and sap our energy to deal with this situation. It strikes at the heart of our true motives to serve Christ and these young people with the grace of God. But there is an antidote!

How to Confidently Identify and Address Scorners and Their Parents—What Forbidden Judging Is and Is Not

There are two things about judging that we need to be clear about in order to address scorners and their parents biblically and wisely.

1. Be clear about what the Scripture does and does not say about judging:

   Judge not, that you be not judged. For with the judgment you pronounce you will be judged, and with the measure you use it will be measured to you. Why do you see the speck that is in your brother's eye, but do not notice the log that is in your own eye? Or how can you say to your brother, 'Let me take the speck out of your eye,' when there is the log in your own eye? You hypocrite, first take the log out of your own eye, and then you will see clearly to take the speck out of your brother's eye. (Matthew 7:1–5)

In this passage, Jesus is not condemning all judgment. He is condemning hypocritical and unmerciful judgment. Just one verse after this paragraph, He urges His disciples to make a very serious judgment with a vivid and, almost, belittling metaphor: "Do not give dogs what is holy, and do not throw your pearls before pigs" (7:6). Is Jesus forgetting what He just commanded in verses 1 through 5? He says do not judge and then tells believers to judge who the spiritual "dogs" and "pigs" are and to not even give them the pearls of the gospel.

There is no inconsistency here. Jesus did not forget what He had just said about judging. He was not forbidding all judging in one breath and then saying the opposite in the next. The log and speck metaphors make it plain that he is forbidding hypocritical judgment. Likewise, the "measure you use" speaks about the spirit of mercy that He commends and the harsh, insensitive judgment that He condemns. All of life includes judgments that believers are commanded to make about others. Jesus is concerned about the way believers go about it. Other passages, such as the ones below, illustrate some of the ways Christians are commanded and advised to be discerning and to make judgments of others.

Whoever walks with the wise becomes wise, but the companion of fools will suffer harm. (Proverbs 13:20)

But now I am writing to you not to associate with anyone who bears the name of brother if he is guilty of sexual immorality or greed, or is an idolater, reviler, drunkard, or swindler—not even to eat with such a one. (1 Corinthians 5:11)

Do not be unequally yoked with unbelievers.
(2 Corinthians 6:14)

Similarly, consider the hundreds of decisions, which often include judgments of others, that the sages of Proverbs advise young people to make in order to be wise. For example, 23:9 urges, "Do not speak in the hearing of a fool, for he will despise the good sense of your words."

Jesus said in John 7:24, "Do not judge by appearances, but judge with right judgment." He is not saying that all judgment is forbidden. Believers are to avoid passing judgment that is hypocritical, unmerciful, hasty, uninformed, and prejudicial.

This brings us to the topic at hand—confronting the scorners and/or their parents. In view of Jesus' counsel, it must be done fairly, humbly, mercifully, firmly, and with specificity. But most important, it must be done.

> 2. Judge what you can see in terms of the scorner's behavior and the impact or effect he or she is having on others.

To be honest, none of us can see the heart of anyone else. We do not know that the young person *is* a scorner at heart. We can only see the outside behavior that the young person displays and then surmise what is going on inside. But the outside is enough for us to use to make a prudent judgment. All of Scripture affirms that outward behavior is fair game for accountability. The Scriptures expect us to judge what we can see, not speculate about what we cannot know absolutely.

With the above guidelines in mind, you might assess the situation with Tom as follows: "Tom sits in the back row in chapel, slouches, snickers, talks, and makes noises while the worship team and speakers address the group. Nearly all he does is under his breath and sneaky. What makes it worse is that Tom's attitude draws others into this same behavior. When I speak to him about his behavior, he just rolls his eyes and denies everything I say that I see. The anger that shows on his face and in the tone of his voice projects a patronizing and disrespectful spirit. It's as though he's saying, 'I don't have to listen to you. You're stupid. I'm going to do what I want, and you can't stop me.' Tom may not be a scorner at heart; I can't see that deeply. And I may not be interpreting everything exactly as it is. I'm not even saying he's the worst or the only one with this problem. But his attitudes and influence on others are certainly like those the Bible describes the scorner as having, and we must hold him accountable for them."

When you or the administrator speaks to Tom or his parents with these themes in mind, your story cannot be contradicted. You are expressing what you are seeing. Parents cannot deny what your experience is. They cannot say, "No, you really don't see him doing that or having that impact." The parents may disagree that these things are as serious as you think they are, or they may disagree with your interpretation of what you see, but these are different matters. The amount and kind of treatment the Scriptures give to the topic underscores how serious it is, whether the parents want to admit the destructive character of Tom's attitude. And the data that you have observed for yourself and that you have collected from others who have seen this spirit gives you evidence—more than you wish you had—to affirm that this is Tom's problem.

On the other hand, if you directly accuse Tom of *being* a scorner *at heart,* you might start a "no, he's not/yes, he is" type of debate. Neither you nor his parents can see his heart. Both of you would be arguing about something that you cannot prove. Judge what you can see, and express your thoughts about Tom in light of those patterns. Avoid accusing Tom of *being* something that you cannot prove him to be. At best, such judgments, even if they are right, will usually lead to angry and disagreeable discussions. In addition to creating more heat than light, these charges often leave the parents and the student with lots of ground to blame the teacher, the school, the administrator, or others for some level of unreasonableness or unfairness. Parents can always find others—such as youth leaders, Sunday school teachers, Christian employers, neighbors—who will vouch for their son's or daughter's good example and attitudes. Young people can turn this spirit on or off when it suits them. Stay with the observed behavior. Stay away from labeling or accusing the student of *being* a particular kind of person.

The Parameters of a Plan

Two passages of Scripture give us parameters for any plan of discipline or accountability that we construct:

> If your brother sins against you, go and tell him his fault, between you and him alone. If he listens to you, you have gained your brother. But if he does not listen, take one or two others along with you, that every charge may be established by the evidence of two or three witnesses. If he refuses to listen to them, tell it to the church. And if he refuses to listen even to the church, let him be to you as a Gentile and a tax collector. (Matthew 18:15–17)

> As for a person who stirs up division, after warning him once and then twice, have nothing more to do with him, knowing that such a person is warped and sinful; he is self-condemned. (Titus 3:10–11)

Did you notice the difference between these two passages? Matthew seems to urge a protracted process. Go alone. In private, talk to the one who has offended you. Then, it seems that you are to give the offender some time to process what you said to him or her. Let the person think it over and respond. If he or she repents, that's great! You have won your brother or sister back. If the person does not repent, go to him or her again. This time take someone else with you to bring the weight of a witness into the picture. This is to help the person think about the seriousness of his or her behavior. Again, there seems to be a patient willingness to let some time go by. There does not seem to be a hurried effort here. This same approach is repeated with more intensity if the person does not repent. Go with two or three others and then, if the offender is still unrepentant, take the concern to the church. The fact that we are given a goal of getting the person to think and repent and that we are told to do so while following steps that involve several others implies that this process includes love, patience, and time for reflection by the offender. Eventually, if the offender does not repent, the church is to put the person out of the fellowship and treat him or her as an unbeliever—regardless of his or her profession of faith. The person has dug his or her heels in and, by having an unrepentant spirit, is acting like an unbeliever.

In contrast, the Titus passage has an unmistakable urgency. You are to warn the offender "once and then twice," and then you are to "have nothing more to do" with him or her. The two passages are not in conflict with each other. They are dealing with two different situations. The Matthew passage gives counsel for a situation in which one person offends another. The sinned-against person, in that case, is to go in private and take the time to seek reconciliation. But the counsel of Paul to Titus is different because the situation is different. The offender to whom Paul refers is sowing discord and division in the church. It is *not* a personal offense that can be patiently endured and treated with long-suffering. The longer this person is allowed to continue his or her behavior, the more and more division he or she will sow. That is exactly what the situation is like with the scorner. The oppressive spirit and negative influence of the scorner greatly outweighs any private personal offense against another. Therefore, addressing the scorner must not be hurried, yet it must not be dragged out over a long period either.

A Plan to Administer Timely, Loving, Humble, and Firm Discipline

From the passages above, we can glean some wise parameters for a plan to work with the scorner.

First, when you become concerned about the student's attitude, you should speak to the student in private. In this meeting, you should express concern about what you sense the student's attitude to be and the behaviors that communicate it. You should also note, in your judgment, the effect the student's attitude seems to be having on others.

Let's apply this method to our situation with Tom. After the other students have left the room, you approach Tom and, in a kind and gracious tone, say, "Tom, thanks for staying after class for a minute, as I asked. I'm deeply concerned about the way you respond when I correct you in class. You slouch, roll your eyes, sigh, and usually end with a smirk and a glance around the room as though you want to make sure some of the others see that you are not going to respect me or do what I ask. This spirit has been growing in you for a while, Tom. But my concern is that I think it is affecting the atmosphere of the class. Others seem to be imitating some of your facial and posture reactions to things I say in class that they don't seem to like. Do you have any idea what I'm talking about, Tom?"

Tom may or may not agree that your observations are accurate. Most often, he will at least deny that this is what he *means* to be doing. He might say you are misunderstanding him. In any case, regardless of his response, you need to assert that his behavior (slouching, sighing, rolling his eyes, glancing around the room, and smirking) needs to change. Describe the alternative behavior that you need to see. You should explain that he should sit up when you speak to him, and he should say, "Yes, Mrs. Smith," or something to that effect, or simply sit up and focus on the class work at hand. If he is corrected, he needs to make the changes the teacher suggests or respectfully ask for a chance to explain what is going on. The rolling eyes and other behaviors must stop.

Second, if the behavior has not changed after two or three days, talk to the student again in private. Remind the student about the conversation you had with him or her a few days earlier. Review the ongoing behaviors of disrespect that you have witnessed and the ways you have seen them affect the class. This review may be simply a rehash of what you said earlier. Indicate that he or she must change and that you will look for that change in the next two days. Tell the student that if you do not see a change, things may become uncomfortable for him or her. Inform the student that you will begin dealing with this situation more seriously by calling his or her parents about your concern.

Third, this is the time to begin asking other teachers whether they are sensing this problem in the student. It is likely that you are not the only teacher who is seeing the student's attitude. I will address more of this topic in the next chapter. It is true that students can turn this spirit on and off. Some exhibit it with just female teachers, some with just male teachers. Some show it with older or younger teachers, some with Bible teachers, and some with teachers who are stricter than others are.

The point here is that it is wise to check with others as a self-check on your own motives and objectivity. If you are the only teacher who is sensing the student's scornful spirit, it would be good to have some others observe what is going on in class. The student may indeed be a scorner. It is rare, though, for this disposition to show up with only one teacher.

Some people may object to consulting with other teachers. They may think of it as a form of gossip. It would be gossip if the goal of the discussion were to complain, criticize, or put down the student. But, just as parents consult with each other about how to help their children, teachers or other professionals have the same obligation to work together and to not judge according to appearance but to "judge with right judgment." They, too, must get the facts by talking to each other.

Fourth, if the behavior does not change after four days, call the student's mother or father about his or her behavior. Then inform your principal about what has been happening and what steps you have taken to address the problem. You may want to invite the parents to come in to talk about the situation if you sense that they are not getting the picture over the phone.

Fifth, if the behavior continues or subsides briefly and then reemerges, talk to the student again and ask the principal to meet with the two of you to assert that the student must change! Note that this meeting with the principal is not a fact-finding tour. Teachers should communicate clearly with the principal about this matter before the meeting. This meeting is not an occasion during which the principal is trying to find out *if* the teacher is reading the situation rightly. The principal is not refereeing at this point, and he or she needs to trust the teacher's judgment. If the principal has doubts about the teacher's judgment, he or she should address that issue before the meeting with the teacher and the student. The purpose of this meeting is for the teacher to clarify the student's behaviors that communicate a scornful attitude and influence others. The principal's role at this stage should be to support the teacher's demand that the behaviors change and to affirm that if they do not change, action that is more drastic will have to be taken.

A Caution for All Teachers!

Teachers beware! Before going down the path of formal confrontation with the scorner in the presence of the principal, you must be certain that your principal is on board, that is, that he or she thinks these attitude matters are as serious as you do. If the principal does not have the same conviction about the matter, or if he or she does not trust your judgment, you will not have his or her unreserved support. And if, after meeting with the student, you walk out of the principal's office without his or her unreserved support, the scorner will be gloating and will be emboldened to strut his or her stuff with even more vigor than when you went into the principal's office. If you think you had a scorner when you went into the principal's office, you haven't seen anything yet!

Sixth, if the behavior does not change within a few more days, the principal should call a meeting with the parent and student as well as the teacher or teachers who are concerned about the needed change. In this meeting, the principal summarizes the issues and announces that the student is officially on disciplinary probation. The student has three weeks in which to make the changes that have been urged in the past by the teacher directly to the student, communicated to the parents by the teacher, and echoed again by the principal in the meeting with the teacher and the student.

Seventh, if there is no change, the formal action of expulsion should occur. In anticipation of this action, it would be wise for the principal to take whatever steps are necessary to be sure that this disciplinary action can be executed promptly. Each day that this person is in your student community, the sourness of the atmosphere continues to undermine the mission and ministry of many. This person is not benign. If the Scriptures are accurate, this malignancy is real, and metastasizing is occurring daily.

Some Procedural Wisdom

1. Keep current.

The fact that you deal with the problem of the scorner this year does not mean that you will not have to deal with it in the future. Our student body changes every year, and students themselves change. Usually the "strike" or "flog" that has occurred sends shock waves throughout the student body. Others who are dabbling with the same patterns of behavior and attitudes often suppress them—at least for a while: "Strike a scoffer, and the simple will learn prudence" (Proverbs 19:25). You probably will not have to address the matter again for a year or more.

In addition to the fear that motivates some students to repress a scornful spirit, the testimony of many who have applied these principles is that the students who do know the Lord often become more confident and expressive:

> When the righteous triumph, there is great glory, but when the wicked rise, people hide themselves. (Proverbs 28:12)

> When the wicked rise, people hide themselves, but when they perish, the righteous increase. (Proverbs 28:28)

There is a refreshing sense that reemerges among the faculty and that flourishes within the student body. The wet blanket has been lifted. Those who were intimidated by the scorner often become boldly righteous in their spirits. This outcome is what we pray for, isn't it? Once they see that this behavior is not going to be mocked, the "righteous" display righteousness without intimidation.

2. Be just.

> A false balance is an abomination to the LORD, but a just weight is his delight. (Proverbs 11:1)

> Unequal weights and unequal measures are both alike an abomination to the LORD. (Proverbs 20:10)

Unequal weights are an abomination to the LORD, and false scales are not good. (Proverbs 20:23)

He has told you, O man, what is good; and what does the LORD require of you but to do justice. (Micah 6:8)

My brothers, show no partiality as you hold the faith in our Lord Jesus Christ.... But if you show partiality, you are committing sin. (James 2:1, 9)

All of the principles for addressing scorners must be applied to any student who displays the characteristics of a scorner and who has the insidious effect of a scorner. You may have to address the child of a teacher, an administrator, a pastor, a board member, or a major donor. Intimidation is a real temptation. But faithfulness to God's rule of justice and righteousness, not the "fear of man" (Proverbs 29:25), must control our decisions.

3. Be expeditious but not precipitous.

Do not drag your feet, and do not jump the gun. Be prompt and efficient but not abrupt and harsh. Do not let this matter drag on with appeal after appeal. Remember, a scorner has a daily impact on your student body (Titus 3:10–11). A scorner might become more aggressive in sowing discord as you begin to bring the weight of accountability upon him or her. This reaction ought to reinforce to you, and all others involved, the kind of person you are truly dealing with:

Whoever corrects a scoffer gets himself abuse. (Proverbs 9:7)

A scoffer does not like to be reproved; he will not go to the wise. (Proverbs 15:12)

Do not be discouraged if you sense that other teachers are not responding with a groundswell of enthusiasm for your concern. The Lord has laid this matter on your heart to address—for His name's sake, for the sake of the Christian education mission, and for this young scorner's sake. Others will support you in this effort, but you may need to be the "point guard" in the effort.

Remember, with this ministry of love and concern, there is going to be pain and suffering in faithfulness. You are in good company if you do not have the wholehearted support of your colleagues. Jesus endured this kind of "hostility against himself." The writer of the book of Hebrews noted this hostility and then urged us to "consider him who endured from sinners such hostility against himself, so that you may not grow weary or fainthearted" (Hebrews 12:3). Not every teacher is ready with the maturity and faith to endure this conflict. But for your faithfulness, you will reap the richness of the harvest that will be illustrated more deeply in the last chapter of this book.

A Final Word About the Outcomes We Are Looking For with This Process

Every Christian educator longs to see heart change in these young people. Clearly, we cannot control whether that happens. Change is ultimately the work of God! But while we cannot insist on conversion or a heart change, we must insist that the young person change the behavior that communicates this destructive disposition. In addition, we must insist that the change occur quickly—noticeably within a day or so. It does not take six months of therapy for a young person to stop smirking, rolling his or her eyes, and sighing.

We deeply want the heart to change in these people, but we cannot see or control that change. We need to pray and love to that end. But in the meantime, faithfulness demands that we hold these young people accountable.

COMMON DIFFICULTIES AND OBJECTIONS WHEN ADDRESSING THESE STUDENTS IN SUCH A SERIOUS WAY

Somewhat predictable negative reactions occur when some in the school community get the sense that you have a plan to actually hold these young people accountable. These reactions may come from colleagues, pastors, or youth leaders within the wider school family. These objections arise sometimes from defensiveness and sometimes from sincere but sentimental misunderstandings of Scripture. Teachers and others who want to address the scorner, out of faithfulness to the Lord, should be alert to the most common reasons and excuses that will be heard for not taking serious action.

I have touched on several of these difficulties and objections in small ways throughout this book. This section is not an exhaustive treatment of any of them, but it does sketch answers that I think are consistent with God's Word for the teacher or administrator who pursues a path of faithfulness with the scorner.

Common Difficulties

1. Parents may be defensive.

Earlier I addressed the obstacle of defensive parents that makes the student's task more difficult and the teacher's task more threatening and painful. Young people do not usually learn their scornful attitudes in a vacuum. Not all children imitate their parents' attitudes.

Sadly, though, it is often true that they do. If this is the case, there may be lots of accusations and insinuations and lots of judging of your motives in the teacher-administrator-parent conference. You may be accused of being unloving, insensitive, judgmental, and maybe of not even being a Christian.

Sometimes parents will be defensive because they are embarrassed. They may feel like failures. They have sensed that teachers are seeing something that they should have been able to correct but have not handled effectively. Sometimes parents need to be encouraged that their parenting has been on track—not perfect, of course. None of us fit that category of parenting. But parents can understand that young people can and do make their own rebellious decisions—in spite of godly parenting. This is why the Old Testament instructs the community as follows: "Whoever curses his father or his mother shall be put to death" (Exodus 21:17). Young people are their own persons and are accountable for their choices—regardless of their parents' effectiveness.

The approach you use in expressing your concern about the young person's attitude is just as important as the concern itself. See the previous section that addresses how to express your judgment of the student who you think is showing signs of being a scorner. Sometimes, parents come to the teacher-administrator-parent conference armed with written testimonials from youth pastors and others to support the upstanding character of their son or daughter. Your affirmation that these testimonials may all be true can be important. You do not have to prove that the student *is* a scorner. You want to see change in what he or she is doing to communicate that spirit in various *school* settings. Students may turn on or off the attitude of contempt toward the authorities in their lives. What you are affirming by addressing this issue as intently as you are, is that the attitude that you and others are sensing must be changed. Any testimonials in hand may be evidence that the student can turn it on or off—when he or she wants to and with whom he or she wants to.

2. Teachers may be sincere but protective, messianic, or simply unaware of the concerns and issues of attitude accountability.

Teachers who you think ought to be your greatest allies may inadvertently help undermine your efforts to hold these young people accountable. Teachers whom the student likes or whose subject the student likes may not readily see this spirit. If other teachers in the school are not on the same page as you are in dealing with this situation, some of their responses can make your efforts much more difficult.

An Accountability Minefield

You have gone through the stages of personally confronting Tom about his attitude, calling his parents, conferring with some of Tom's other teachers, and talking to the principal. Even the principal, Mr. Taylor, has met with Tom and has notified his mother that Tom is on notice to change the scoffing spirit that he exhibits in your class, in chapel, and in Bible class. Today is the meeting that the principal has set up in which he is going to give Tom the ultimatum—change or leave!

The night before the meeting, Tom's mother, Mrs. Smith, called the P.E. teacher, Mr. Jones, whom Tom respects and likes.

"Mr. Jones, I'm wondering if you've noticed whether Tom's attitude is OK and if he is getting along OK with the others and with you in class."

"Yes, Mrs. Smith, Tom is doing fine in P.E. He participates, seems to have a good attitude about the things we do, and cooperates and follows my directions. I like Tom. Why do you ask? Is there a problem?"

"I don't think so," Mrs. Smith replies. "I just wanted to see if you had noticed anything that was troubling to you about Tom. Thank you very much."

The next day, Mrs. Smith arrives for the teacher-administrator-parent conference about Tom. The principal welcomes her into the office, and everyone sits down. The principal prays at the beginning of the conference. Then, as he begins to summarize and explain why all are gathered, Mrs. Smith interrupts politely, yet with a little tone of annoyance in her voice.

"Mr. Taylor, before you begin, I have something to say. I talked to Mr. Jones last night. He is Tom's P.E. teacher. I asked him if Tom has any attitude problems and if he gets along well with the other students. Mr. Jones said that everything is fine with Tom. He has no attitude problem with Tom, and Tom obeys and follows directions in his class. I think there is a problem here, as you said in your call to set up this meeting. But the problem isn't with my son. It's with your teacher. I think this is a personality problem between your teacher and Tom. Since your teacher is the one who is supposed to be more mature and more spiritual, it seems to me that she should be able to deal with this."

Much of the failure for this conference to accomplish what the principal had planned is because of the thoughtless, or at least unguarded, response that Mr. Jones gave to Tom's mother. He was not wrong in what he said, just imprudent.

Here is the way the teacher could have responded more helpfully:
"Mr. Jones, I'm wondering if you've noticed whether Tom's attitude is OK and if he is getting along OK with the others and with you in class."

"Yes, Mrs. Smith. Tom is doing fine in P.E. He participates, seems to have a good attitude about the things we do, and cooperates and follows my directions. I like Tom. But that doesn't necessarily mean that things are going well in other classes for Tom. Tom likes P.E. When students like a subject, they can be very positive. But when they don't like something, they can turn on an attitude. Has there been a concern about Tom's attitude?"

Do you notice the difference in this response? Mr. Jones acknowledges Tom's ability to make good and poor decisions about his attitude and acknowledges the possibility that his colleagues may have noticed something about Tom's attitude that may be true even though he has not seen it.

In your planned efforts to help the faculty and administrative personnel understand the urgency of working with the scorner or mocker in biblical ways, be sure to give attention to faculty member responses. Help faculty members to understand ways they can respond truthfully while respecting the possibility that these young people may present themselves differently with other teachers.

3. Administrators or board members may be intimidated.

"You may talk about Daniel facing the lions, Shadrach and his friends facing the fiery furnace, or Stephen facing his assailants, but you've never faced an incensed parent or a snarling board member!"

This could be the sentiment of an administrator who has just gotten off the phone with an irate parent who is deeply troubled by the call from a teacher about Tom's attitude or, perhaps, by a call from the principal. Near the end of the previous chapter, I cautioned teachers about using these biblical principles to pursue the scorner without having total support from the administrator. Teachers must assess the level of support and the seriousness with which their administrator takes these concerns. Beginning this course of treatment and then backing away from it because the administrator does not support your actions will have a major impact on the faculty's esprit de corps, the student body's respect for authority and righteousness, and the scorner's arrogance and insidious spirit that will continue to spread.

Administrators *do* often face enormous pressures from parents who are defensive of their children. Administrators should base their conviction about the scorner and the scorner's accountability on biblical principle, just as teachers do. Otherwise, administrators may not have the willingness to act on principle. They may be more easily intimidated and back away from biblically required accountability.

Similarly, board members must be supportive of the administration's approach. They need to have been oriented to this problem and to what the Bible teaches about it. If a board has the right to upstage or call into question administrative decisions about the expulsion of students, the board should be informed on the issues at hand. If a board that does not understand the issues pulls the rug out from under an administrator who has begun on this path of adhering to biblical principle, the insidious spirit that the teacher and administrator wanted to dampen will only deepen and become more destructive.

What can teachers or administrators do to bring important support personnel on board with these concerns? Teacher in-service days, school faculty or board retreats, and teacher or administrator conventions may be good opportunities to give biblical research and discussion time to the topic. The idea of holding scorners accountable for their attitudes is not hidden in the Bible. Copies of this book or just a concordance or topical study of scorner and mocker attitudes throughout the Scriptures will establish the urgency of the matter and give clear parameters to develop policies and procedures to address these young people.

Administrator and board member intimidation by an influential parent, a threatened lawsuit, or the pressure of other church or community friends of family members can be very real. Only clarity and confidence in what the Scriptures say about this kind of pressure will give these leaders the courage to be faithful.

4. A scorner may stubbornly deny the "charges" brought against him or her and may manifest an affected disposition of innocence and surprise.

Several years ago, a Philadelphia business executive was caught on videotape taking a bribe from an undercover police officer. The local news media got the videotape and played segments of it while interviewing the business executive. He vigorously denied taking a bribe. The transaction could be seen and heard on the videotape. Clearly, he knew what he was doing. But he denied it. Even in the face of the clearest evidence, he insisted that he did nothing wrong.

Sometimes our students learn to do the same thing. They have witnessed others stonewalling the accusations brought against them and then getting away with it. Students do the same thing and hope for the same results.

Some years ago, I was teaching a Bible class that included three guys whom I was becoming increasingly concerned about because of their attitudes. As the semester wore on, I became more and more aware that I was encountering scoffers, in the Bible's terms. On one occasion, the three came into class and sat with their elbows on their desks, holding their chins in the palms of their hands, with an unmistakable gesture turned in my direction. Their middle fingers were the only fingers running up alongside their cheeks. Their other fingers were folded under their chins. The students were positioned so that I could see their contempt but so that others in the class could not. They kept that posture throughout the entire period—an effort that required an unusual measure of intention.

After the class, I asked all three to stay behind. In retrospect, I see that doing so was probably a mistake. I tried to confront them graciously yet firmly. They, of course, were appalled that I would draw such a conclusion. They said it was just a coincidence and that I was misreading their intent. I insisted that they knew what they were doing, and I indicated that I would be talking further to them and to their parents.

Later, I met with the three of them individually. Two of them caved in somewhat quickly, pleading with me not to call their parents. The third only acknowledged his behavior after my prolonged assertions about what I saw and what the others admitted. Their confessions came only after they became convinced that I was not going to second-guess what I saw and change my story. Their gesture was intentional, but they did everything they could to try to get me to doubt what was plainly in front of me. I was not going to buy their "coincidental" and "we didn't mean anything by it" stories.

Some scorners have learned that if they deny that they have a mocking disposition or if they insist long enough that the teacher is mistaken, teachers will begin to doubt themselves and soften their responses to simple warnings. It is important for us to be thoughtful and not swift to speak. But it is also important for the teachers who want to address this problem to hold firmly to what they have seen and not be put off by strong denials of any intent to do wrong. If it looks like a duck, quacks like a duck, and walks like a duck, it is most likely a duck (adapted from a quote by Richard James Cardinal Cushing). We do not have to be trapped into proving beyond the shadow of a doubt that the student *is* a scorner. We just have to have indications that he or she is communicating that spirit to us and/or to others.

5. Teachers and administrators (any in the loop of concern about these attitude issues) may have their confidence in the clear teaching of Scripture undermined or eroded by psychotherapeutic concerns about self-esteem and broad definitions of "abuse."

Whom do scorners respect? Whose values do scorners esteem? Whose direction are scorners willing to follow? Whose reputation are scorners willing to protect and encourage others to regard? Whose will are scorners open to pleasantly obey? Whom are scorners ready to acknowledge as a rightful authority in their life? Whose authority do scorners recognize to "make" them do anything? There is one common answer to these questions. Scorners care about their own respect, values, direction, reputation, will, and authority. They are really only ready to listen to one person—themselves.

Scorners will not listen to rebuke or correction, and they will not consult with the wise. They delight in putting down those in authority and get satisfaction out of making others look bad. Their problem is not a poor or low self-esteem. In the Bible's terminology, it is quite the opposite: "These are grumblers, malcontents, following their own sinful desires;... 'In the last time there will be scoffers, following their own ungodly passions.' It is these who cause divisions, worldly people, devoid of the Spirit" (Jude 16, 18). If there is any characterization about self-esteem that we can make about scoffers, it is that they have extremely high self-esteem. *Arrogant* is a more accurate biblical term to summarize the disposition of scorners. This is a heart issue: "Everyone who is arrogant in heart is an abomination to the LORD; be assured, he will not go unpunished" (Proverbs 16:5).

Similarly, abuse is not simply hurting someone's feelings. Abuse is real. It has always been condemned by God. But discipline and holding another accountable for his or her choices is not being abusive—especially if the manner of holding the person accountable is also prescribed by Scripture. The verbs of accountability "strike" (Proverbs 19:25), "punished" (Proverbs 21:11), "drive out" (Proverbs 22:10), and "reject" (Titus 3:10, NKJV) point to personal choice that is rooted in a moral orientation, not a psychological inferiority.

Common Objections

1. "Isn't this judging?"

Yes, it is. But as we noted in the last chapter, not all judging is forbidden. Only hypocritical, precipitous, unmerciful judgment is condemned: "Do not judge by appearances, but judge with right judgment" (John 7:24). All of life in general, and the Christian life in particular, includes judgments about people.

Naivety is never esteemed in Scripture: "The simple believes everything, but the prudent gives thought to his steps" (Proverbs 14:15). It is the spirit and manner of judging that must be applied carefully in the case of the scorner. Vindictiveness, anger from being embarrassed by the scorner, and the desire to win a power struggle are never right bases for judging. But advancing righteousness in a righteous way is not only OK, it is commanded.

2. "Isn't it our responsibility to minister to these students? Aren't we really sacrificing these students for our comfort level? Doesn't love mean that we should be long-suffering with them and even endure mistreatment?"

A board member in one Christian school told me that he believed that once a school has accepted a student, the school is making a commitment to stick with that child through thick and thin—until graduation. This was his explanation for why his son should not be expelled, even though his son's behavior had been identified as scornful.

Love and discipline are never portrayed as opposites in the Bible. On the contrary, "the Lord disciplines the one he loves" (Hebrews 12:6). Holding young people accountable, even with painful consequences, is the most loving thing we can do to help them come to their senses:

> Whoever spares the rod hates his son, but he who loves him is diligent to discipline him. (Proverbs 13:24)

> Folly is bound up in the heart of a child, but the rod of discipline drives it far from him. (Proverbs 22:15)

> Do not withhold discipline from a child; if you strike him with a rod, he will not die. If you strike him with the rod, you will save his soul from Sheol. (Proverbs 23:13–14)

The Scriptures say to "drive out" (Proverbs 22:10) the scorner. Sentimentality or warm fuzzy feelings do not trump God's directives. Long-suffering does not mean interminable suffering of behavior that destroys others or the ministry of Christian education for others. Even God in His long-suffering has His limits. Every indication is that we as Christians should have our limits with the scorner also.

Are we sacrificing this student for the welfare of others? In one sense, yes, we are. But it should be clear: either way, we are making a sacrifice. Either we will sacrifice this young person for the sake of others and the ministry, or we will sacrifice others and the ministry for the sake of the scorner. One way or the other, a sacrifice is going to be made. The question is, which one does God implore us to make?

3. "By putting these students out of our school, aren't we saying that God's resources are insufficient for helping them change?"

No, we are not. Would we say the gospel is weak because some people reject it? Of course we would not. Would we say Jesus was ineffective because He was criticized, condemned, and killed? Certainly we would not. The gospel is the "power of God for salvation to everyone who believes" (Romans 1:16), and Jesus "finished" God's mission for Him (John 19:30). The validity of any form of ministry is not determined by how well others accept it. God's guidance and appointment for any feature of ministry are what determine its legitimacy. Faithfulness to His mission is God's criteria for effectiveness (Matthew 25:21, 23; 1 Corinthians 4:2). We long to see God's grace being received by others through our ministries. But it is still true that "we are the aroma of Christ to God among those who are being saved and among those who are perishing, to one a fragrance from death to death, to the other a fragrance from life to life. Who is sufficient for these things?" (2 Corinthians 2:15–16).

We are not limiting the power of God by removing students who are unwilling to change their scornful spirit. On one hand, we are recognizing the realness of choices that young people make, and on the other hand, we are affirming that the consequences of their attitude and behavioral choices are not in their control. Young people, by their creation in the image of God, make authentic decisions. They are not robots. Because of this realness, they are accountable for their decisions to God and others whom God designates as authorities in their lives.

4. "What about the damage we may do to these students' self-esteem?"

Difficulty number 5 in the previous section addresses this question. Also, see *When People Are Big and God Is Small* by Edward Welch (1997).

The real issue is one of hope, not good feelings about oneself. Because of God's work in Christ and His assurances and promises in Christ, believers have a hope that gives them indomitable motivation. It is not *self-esteem* but *confidence in Christ's purpose* that transcends criticisms, put-downs, slightings, misjudgments, abuses, injustices, oppressions, exploitations, betrayals, insensitivities, disadvantages, failures, and every other kind of wrong that we may suffer at the hands of others. In addition, this confidence in Christ even transcends our own sins and failures: "For we are his workmanship, created in Christ Jesus for good works, which God prepared beforehand, that we should walk in them" (Ephesians 2:10). Excusing scornful behavior, or allowing it to go unaddressed because of self-esteem issues, elevates psychotherapeutic concerns above biblical ones.

5. "What lesson are we teaching about forgiveness in the Christian community if we expel these students?"

We had a vivid lesson about the way our modern culture has muddied the idea of forgiveness when President Clinton was frustrated because people wanted to hold him accountable for his immorality and lying, even though he "apologized to the nation." In so many words, he was saying that if he says he is sorry, he is supposed to be exonerated. He expected people to forgive and forget and, subsequently, negate any consequences. The Bible is clear that we are to forgive any offenses and not be bitter or resentful:

> Whenever you stand praying, forgive, if you have anything against anyone, so that your Father also who is in heaven may forgive you your trespasses. (Mark 11:25)

> Let all bitterness and wrath and anger and clamor and slander be put away from you, along with all malice. (Ephesians 4:31)

But forgiveness does not negate disciplinary action or the stiff consequences for hurtful or destructive decisions. Hebrews 12:11 makes it clear that though He has forgiven, the Father still disciplines His children with "painful" discipline. Forgiveness and accountability are not mutually exclusive. In fact, the willingness of the community to love and accept the return of such a student, after a pattern of genuine repentance, may rightly be part of any imposed disciplinary action.

6. "We are ignoring reality if we deal with the problem this way. We live in a sinful world, and this approach seems to forget that we need to be willing to serve in a fallen world."

We certainly do live in a sinful world. But God has given His Word to be followed by fallen people who live in a sinful world. The Bible is not a collection of platitudes for an ideal society in a future heaven that will be devoid of sin. It is to be applied now by sinners who struggle with the same problems that all other sinners have. The Bible is meant to be used now, in "the present evil age" (Galatians 1:4), with humility and a concern for righteousness. We are far from ignoring reality when we obey God's principles for holding the scorner accountable; we are affirming the relevance and applicability of God's Word for making "the man of God"—including the Christian school teacher, administrator, or board member— "competent, equipped for every good work" (2 Timothy 3:17; note the ministry context in this verse).

THE FRUIT OF FAITHFULNESS
IN MANY SCHOOLS

Any school community would be a more pleasant place without negativity, mockery, cynicism, bitterness, disrespect, division, and anger. But addressing the scorner in God's way does more than eliminate a destructive, heavy spirit. It encourages a wide range of opposite nurturing qualities:

> When a scoffer is punished, the simple becomes wise.
> (Proverbs 21:11)

> Drive out a scoffer, and strife will go out, and quarreling and abuse will cease. (Proverbs 22:10)

After I had been in one Christian school for about thirteen years, the student editor for the school newspaper asked me to write an article about the spiritual transformation that I had witnessed taking place in the student body during the previous five years. There had been a radical change in the school atmosphere. It had begun, in my judgment, because God had blessed the school for its faithful, though painful, application of His directives for addressing the mockers and scoffers in our school. The administration had been boldly supportive of teachers who championed God's warnings and instructions about putting such people "out." That action began a cascade of spiritual life that was at its peak when the newspaper editor asked me to write about what I had seen. The following is the article that I wrote:

"See What God Has Done"
by Dr. Rick Horne

The stage in the Journey Gym was full. STARS, the student-teacher talent night, had moved along entertainingly. A choral group was set to sing a selection that expressed uncompromised commitment to the Lord. A teacher turned my way and saw tears in my eyes. I said, "How I long that the love for God expressed in those words would be more than empty, hollow sounds."

My colleague nodded in sad agreement. What had been entertaining up to that point became a painful reminder that spiritual desire had little place of importance for the vast majority of our students. It had been this way for my eight years there.

That was five years ago, but look at what God has been doing since then. Spiritually minded leaders have emerged with boldness in many high school classes. There are Bible studies that are planned, promoted, and led by students. Upper-class students have sought to show spiritual concern to underclassmen through the Big Brother Big Sister program. Students participate in major ways in our weekly chapels. Students can be heard talking about personal devotional time and witnessing opportunities. They can be seen putting their arms around the shoulders of a troubled friend while inviting him or her to pray.

Student leaders have bound themselves together to struggle with ideas and plans for stimulating greater school spiritual-mindedness: The high school retreats, field days, and gym nights have clear spiritual features. Our athletic teams, student publications, and leadership groups exhibit motives that are higher than personal glory.

It is hard to believe that almost none of these evidences of spiritual growth were present five years ago. The glow of life here at that time was very dim.

> Tears come to my eyes when I think about how I've been
> here for thirteen years now and the crescendo of spiritual
> life here over the last four or five years has been among the
> most thrilling works of God I've ever observed. (*The
> Crusader*, November 1984)

Obviously, there is no guarantee that God will do this same thing in every situation where faithful people choose to obey God's wise counsel about the scorner and mocker. But He does bless obedience, often with prosperity: "If you are wise, your wisdom will reward you" (Proverbs 9:12, NIV).

To those who would practice God's wisdom, in this situation and any area in which He provides it, the sage of Proverbs says, "Long life is in her right hand; in her left hand are riches and honor. Her ways are ways of pleasantness, and all her paths are peace. She is a tree of life to those who lay hold of her; those who hold her fast are called blessed" (Proverbs 3:16–18).

When the scorner is addressed God's way, there is an absence of the scorner's spirit and his or her many subtle, undermining, destructive effects. This faithfulness may also create the fertile soil for your many spiritual efforts, prayers, and sacrifices to be used by God to grow a spirit that is open to correction, positive about education, and respectful of God and all who represent Him: "When a scoffer is punished, the simple becomes wise" (Proverbs 21:11).

Soli Deo Gloria

APPENDIX

Helps to Identify Scorners and Mockers:
A Checklist of Specific Verbal and Nonverbal Behaviors to Document a Pattern of Scorning

Scorners and mockers are people who display an attitude of contempt for God, His Word, and other authority figures whom God commands people to hold in high regard. These attitudes are patterns that commonly show up toward teachers, administrators, and even students whose standards are a reproof to the scorner. Ultimately, it is God's authority that is being rejected by the scorner.

Teachers and parents must identify student behaviors that convey a scornful, mocking, or scoffing contempt. You cannot judge students' hearts infallibly. You can detect behaviors that look like those of the scorner and mocker, that communicate this spirit to you, and that have the effect on others that the Bible describes scorners as having.

The following list is not exhaustive, but it specifies some common ways teachers and others have seen students exhibit a scornful, scoffing, mocking disposition. Not one of these manifestations is, in itself, an indication of a scornful attitude. Teachers should note *patterns* of these traits in students over several weeks and throughout various classes and settings (e.g., chapel, class meetings, classes in which the Bible is used, venues in which there is opportunity for student contributions). These observations will give teachers, administrators, and parents the needed specifics to hold students accountable for doing things that communicate these unacceptable attitudes. They will also give administrators specifics for needed student changes that they require as part of the discipline process.

Nonverbal Communication Pattern	Example/Incident in Which It Is Displayed
rolling eyes	
a sigh, a breath of disgust/contempt (often accompanies the rolling eyes)	
the silent treatment when being addressed	
avoidance of eye contact when being spoken to	
a smirk or patronizing smile	
stubbornness	
an angry glare	
slouching defiance	
disruptive, annoying noises	

Verbal Communication Patterns

Example /Incident in Which It Is Displayed

arrogant tone of voice   _____

insulting speech   _____

disobedience   _____

uncooperativeness   _____

slander   _____

hateful tone of voice   _____

disrespectful "why"   _____

gossip   _____

contempt   _____

sneering speech   _____

patronizing speech   _____

disrespectful speech   _____

sarcastic speech   _____

rude speech   _____

derisive speech   _____

derogatory speech   _____

disparaging speech   _____

digs   _____

lies   _____

other verbal/behavioral forms   _____

REFERENCES

Kidner, Derek. 1964. *Proverbs.* Downers Grove, IL: InterVarsity Press.

Ross, Allan. 1991. *The expositor's Bible commentary,* vol. 5, *Psalms, Proverbs, Ecclesiastes, Song of Songs.* Ed. Frank E. Gabelein. Grand Rapids, MI: Zondervan Publishing House.

Welch, Edward. 1997. *When people are big and God is small.* Phillipsburg, NJ: Presbyterian & Reformed Publishing.

INDEX OF SCRIPTURE USED